JESUS:
LESSONS IN LOVE

How To Love God,
Love Others And
Love Yourself More

ERIC ELDER

Jesus: Lessons In Love is part of a series of
inspirational resources produced by Eric
Elder Ministries. For a boost in your
faith anytime, please visit:
WWW.THERANCH.ORG

Cover image provided by Michael Swanson.
http://blogs.msdn.com/mswanson/
articles/wallpaper.aspx

ISBN 978-1-931760-25-6

DEDICATION

To all those who need a touch from Christ—
expressed, perhaps, through you.

ACKNOWLEDGMENTS

Special thanks to my wife, Lana, for reading and revising each of these devotionals, infusing them with additional spiritual insights and practical wisdom.

THE GREATEST COMMANDMENT

Scripture Reading: Matthew 22:37-39

I've been wrestling with something I recently heard and I'd like to share it with you. I wonder if it affects you like it affects me:

> *"If you're not close to people who are far from God, you're probably not as close to God as you think you are."*

I don't know about you, but that makes me squirm a little bit. I've been a Christian for over twenty years. I run an Internet ministry that reaches thousands of people a month. I've been the president of our local ministers' association for several years. But if I were to judge my relationship with God by how close I am to people who are far from Him, I don't know that I'd score very high.

I want to win people to Christ. I want to make a difference in the world. But I can't say that I always want to do what it takes to love people the way Christ loved them.

I was reading a letter recently from a man who actually had Jesus over to his house for dinner. It was written by a man named Matthew. He was a tax collector who lived at the same time as Jesus.

It must have been as much of a surprise to Matthew as it was to everyone else in town when Jesus walked up to Matthew and said, "Follow me." Matthew ended up hosting a banquet at his house for Jesus.

The religious leaders were outraged. They questioned some of Jesus' followers:

> *"Why does your teacher eat with tax collectors and 'sinners'?"*
> *On hearing this, Jesus said, "It is not the healthy who need a doctor, but the sick. But go and learn what this means: 'I desire mercy, not sacrifice.' For I have not come to call the righteous, but sinners"* *(Matthew 9:9-13).*

I love Jesus' response. But it nails me as much as it nailed the religious leaders of that day. I don't want to be a Pharisee, a Saducee, or any other kind of "-see." I want to be like Jesus.

I want to learn how to love God more. I want to learn how to love people more. And I want to learn how to love myself more.

These are, according to Jesus, the greatest of commandments:

> *"'Love the Lord your God with all your heart and with all your soul and with all your mind.' This is the first and greatest commandment. And the second is like it: 'Love your neighbor as yourself'" (Matthew 22:37-39).*

Jesus gave us the best example for how to live out these commandments. That's why I'm going to be reading Matthew's letter again and again in the days ahead. Matthew covers the life of Jesus in 28 chapters, from the foretelling of His birth to His death and resurrection. Not only did Matthew have Jesus over for dinner, but he went on to spend the next three years of his life with Jesus, day and night.

Matthew watched how Jesus loved people, healed people, forgave people, taught people. Matthew watched as Jesus prayed to God, pleaded with God, submitted to God. Matthew watched as Jesus responded to His critics, walked away from His critics, and was eventually killed by His critics. And Matthew watched as people loved Jesus, adored Jesus, and gave up their lives for Jesus.

I love Matthew's letter for a number of reasons, not the least of which is that I put my faith in Christ twenty years ago while reading about Him in Matthew's letter. I'm so thankful that Jesus went out of His way to love people who didn't yet believe in Him, who didn't yet trust in Him, who didn't yet live their lives for Him.

I'm so thankful because I'm one of those people. And I want to be just like Him.

I hope you'll join me in the days ahead as I take a closer look, page by page through Matthew's letter, at how we can all be more like Jesus, starting next time with Chapter 1.

I also want to encourage you to read each day's Scripture Reading in your own Bible in addition to my devotional for that day. I've limited myself to touching upon just one thought in each chapter of Matthew, but there's so much God may speak to you about other subjects in your life. When you're done reading all the daily Scripture Readings, you'll have read through the entire book of Matthew.

And finally, I've included a prayer at the end of each devotional to help you focus your own prayers by praying them along with me. Here's today's prayer.

PRAYER: FATHER, HELP ME TO BE MORE LIKE JESUS SO THAT I CAN LOVE YOU, LOVE OTHERS AND LOVE MYSELF MORE. IN JESUS' NAME, AMEN.

Lesson 1

How To Begin
Loving Others More

Scripture Reading: Matthew 1

J esus told a story about two people...one who loved much, and one who loved little. It's a story that I'm particularly interested in because I want to learn how to truly love God and love others more. But how? Where do I start in my desire to be more loving? I believe Jesus tells us in this story.

He told it while at a dinner party at the home of a religious leader. A woman who had lived a sinful life came into the house to find Jesus. She fell at His feet, weeping and wetting His feet with her tears, then pouring some perfume on His feet and wiping them with her hair.

The man who had invited Jesus to dinner was outraged, not so much at the woman, but at Jesus, who would allow such a sinful woman to touch Him. So Jesus said to the man:

"Simon, I have something to tell you."

"Tell me teacher," he said.

"Two men owed money to a certain moneylender. One owed him five hundred denarii, [a danarius was a coin worth about a day's wages] and the other fifty. Neither of them had the money to pay him back, so he canceled the debts of both. Now which of them will love him more?"

Simon replied, "I suppose the one who had the bigger debt canceled."

"You have judged correctly," Jesus said.

Then he turned toward the woman and said to Simon, "Do you see this woman? I came into your house. You did not give me any water for my feet, but she wet my feet with her tears and wiped them with her hair. You did not give me a kiss, but this woman, from the time I entered, has not stopped kissing my feet. You did not put oil on my head, but she has poured perfume on my feet. Therefore, I tell you, her many sins have been forgiven—for she loved much. But he who has been forgiven little loves little" (Luke 7:40-47).

Here's what I get from this story: the amount of love we have for God and for others is directly related to how much we have been forgiven.   If we have been forgiven much, we will love much, but if we have been forgiven little, we will love little.

So how can I begin to grow in my love for God and for others? Sin more, so I can love more? I don't think so! I think the place to begin is to realize how very much we have already been forgiven.

How much is that? Enough for God to send Jesus to earth to die in our place for the sins we've committed.

This is where the book of Matthew starts. After giving us a detailed genealogy of where Jesus came from, Matthew tells us what Jesus came for. The angel who spoke to Joseph said it best:

> *"Joseph son of David, do not be afraid to take Mary home as your wife, because what is conceived in her is from the Holy Spirit. She will give birth to a son, and you are to give him the name Jesus, because he will save his people from their sins"* *(Matthew 1:20b-21).*

Jesus came to save us from our sins. God loved us so much that He didn't want us to die because of all that we had done wrong. If our sins were serious enough for Jesus to have to die for them, they must be terribly grievous to God. And if that's true, then each of us have already been forgiven much.

We don't have to sin more to be forgiven of more in order to love more. We just need to realize how much we've already sinned, how much we've already been forgiven, and how much we've already been loved by God. Once we realize that, I believe that love will naturally flow out from within us, like tears mixed with perfume and poured out at Jesus' feet.

PRAYER: FATHER, HELP US REALIZE HOW MUCH YOU'VE LOVED US AND FORGIVEN US, SO THAT WE CAN LOVE YOU AND LOVE OTHERS MORE. IN JESUS' NAME, AMEN.

SEEING PEOPLE
AS GOD SEES THEM

Scripture Reading: Matthew 2

Part of loving others involves seeing people as God sees them. Sometimes that takes more effort than other times!

One of the hardest, but most rewarding, parts of my ministry, is listening to people as they share some of their deepest personal sins they've committed, and listening to the pain that it's caused them, God and others. It's hard, because I'm torn between wanting to cry and wanting to run away as they pour out things that are truly unsettling. But it's rewarding, because I know that their confession often leads to greater healing than they've ever known before. As the Bible says:

"Therefore confess your sins to each other and pray for each other so that you may be healed" (James 5:16a).

But in the midst of listening to people confess their sins, I'm also torn in another way: I'm torn in my feelings towards them as people. I want to love them, but because of what they're telling me, I sometimes wonder how I can. How can God do it? How can He continue loving people, knowing what they've done? And how can I?

Matthew 2 gives me a clue: God loves people because He sees their lives from beginning to end. He created them. He knows them intimately. And He sees them not only for what they are, but also for what they are to become.

The verses in Matthew 2 show us how much care God took to see that Jesus was born, in the right place, at the right time, and how much God was involved in moving Jesus through those early years of His life in ways that kept Him alive and on course to fulfill the purposes for which God sent Him to earth.

- *Micah foretold, hundreds of years before Jesus was born, that Jesus would be born in Bethlehem (see Micah 5:2).*
- *Hosea foretold that Jesus would later return*

from Egypt, saying, "Out of Egypt I called my son" (Hosea 11:1).

- *Jeremiah foretold that there would be suffering back in Bethlehem on account of Christ, saying there would be "weeping and great mourning" (Jeremiah 31:15).*

If God knew these things about Jesus' life, but no one elses's, I might not be convinced that God takes the same care with each of us. But God knows each of us just as intimately, and has unique purposes for each of our lives.

- *David says: "All the days ordained for me were written in Your book before one of them came to be" (Psalm 139:16b).*
- *God told Jeremiah: "Before I formed you in the womb I knew you, before you were born I set you apart; I appointed you as a prophet to the nations" (Jeremiah 1:5).*
- *Isaiah said: "Before I was born the Lord called me; from my birth he has made mention of my name" (Isaiah 49:1b).*

And God foretold the births of people like Isaac and John the Baptist, even before they were conceived:

- *"Then the LORD said, 'I will surely return to you about this time next year, and Sarah your wife will have a son'" (Genesis 18:10).*
- *"Your wife Elizabeth will bear you a son, and you are to give him the name John" (Luke 1:13b).*

God knows each one of us, intimately, and He loves each one of us, even when we mess up terribly. I think part of the reason is that He has the ability to see our lives from beginning to end.

That's a good reminder for me when I see someone in the midst of their sin. If I can see them as God sees them, then I'll be much more likely to truly love them, and to truly help them get back on track with God's plans for their lives.

Although I don't naturally have the ability to see people as God sees them, I know God can give me that ability if I ask Him for it, the ability see people as He sees them, so I can love them as He loves them.

PRAYER: FATHER, HELP ME SEE PEOPLE AS YOU SEE THEM, SO I CAN LOVE THEM AS YOU LOVE THEM. IN JESUS' NAME, AMEN.

Lesson 3

LOVING OTHERS
AS GOD LOVES THEM

Scripture Reading: Matthew 3

I have a question for you. There's a point in Jesus' life where God's love for His Son, Jesus, is so full, that God speaks these words from heaven so that all those around Jesus can hear:

> *"This is my Son, whom I love, with Him I am well-pleased."*

The question is this: At what point in Jesus' life does God speak these words? Was it:

A) After Jesus had just healed someone who was sick?
B) After He walked on water?
C) After He had raised someone from the dead?
D) After He had preached a life-changing message to a massive crowd?
E) None of the above.

If you answered, "E) None of the above," you're right. The point at which God vocalized His tremendous love for His Son wasn't after Jesus did any of these things. It takes place before every one of them. In fact, it takes place before Jesus did even one recorded miracle, or one recorded act of service to anyone else. It takes place in Matthew chapter 3, when Jesus came to John to be baptized by Him:

> *"As soon as Jesus was baptized, he went up out of the water. At that moment heaven was opened, and he saw the Spirit of God descending like a dove and lighting on him. And a voice from heaven said, 'This is my Son, whom I love; with him I am well pleased.'" (Matthew 3:16-17).*

God loved Jesus right from the beginning of Jesus' ministry, not just at the end of it. What does this say about God's love for us and for others? Is God's love the same for us, or was it different for Jesus, because Jesus was, after all, sinless!

As a father myself, I believe God's love for us begins way before we would even think it would. My oldest daughter turned sixteen this weekend. I remember the sense of love I began to feel for her in those first moments after her birth, and then in those first days, those first weeks, and those first months as a baby. Right from the start I felt an overwhelming love for her, even though she hadn't yet done one spectacular thing for me or for anyone else. In fact, about all she did was eat, sleep, cry, and make messes that we had to clean up. But my love for her was unmeasurable.

I'm sure my love for my daughter is just a fraction of the kind of love God has for each one of us. Even before we could ever possibly do one miracle in His name, or one act of kindness, or one good deed for someone else, God loves us.

Even when all we can do is eat, sleep, cry, and make messes that He has to clean up, God loves us. Even though we're not anywhere close to being sinless, like Jesus was, God loves us. The Bible says:

> *"But God demonstrates his own love for us in this: While we were still sinners, Christ died for us"* *(Romans 5:8).*

God loves us, even though we sin. That's why He sent Jesus to die in our place. God isn't waiting for you to do something spectacular before He loves you. He loves you right now, this very minute.

If we want to love others the way that God loves them, then we need to set our hearts on loving them before they ever do even one good deed. We need to commit to loving them even when all they might do is eat, sleep, cry, and make messes that we have to clean up. We need to keep loving them, even when they sin. For when we can have a love like that in our hearts for others, then we'll be able to truly begin to love them as God loves them.

PRAYER: FATHER, HELP ME TO HAVE A HEART LIKE YOURS, A HEART THAT LOVES OTHERS FOR NO OTHER REASON THAN THE FACT THAT YOU CREATED THEM AND THAT YOU LOVE THEM, EVEN WHEN THEY MESS UP. IN JESUS' NAME, AMEN.

WHAT WOULD
JESUS PREACH?

Scripture Reading: Matthew 4

J esus preached many things, but in Matthew
chapter 4, I'm struck by one of the very
first messages Jesus preached. While it
was a message of love, Jesus didn't start off
with the words, "Love one another," or "Do
to others what you would have them do to
you." Here's the way Jesus began his preaching ministry:

"Repent, for the kingdom of heaven is near"
(Matthew 4:17).

To some people, that may not sound like a
very loving message for the beginning of a
ministry. But from God's point of view, it's
one of the most loving messages we could
hear ourselves, or share with others: "Repent,
for the kingdom of heaven is near." Just as
John the Baptist pleaded with people to repent, to turn away from their sins, Jesus con-

tinued preaching this same message after John was put in prison.

Jesus, of all people, knew how destructive sin is in people's lives. It's so destructive that God sent Jesus to die for our sins so that we wouldn't have die for them ourselves. But even though Jesus would eventually pay the ultimate price for our sins, He still called for people to repent. Why? Because Jesus knew that our sins don't only effect us for our eternal life, but they also effect us for our life here on earth.

If the Bible is true when it says that "the wages of sin is death" (Romans 3:23), as I believe it is, then calling people to turn away from their sins so that they can have life is one of the most loving messages we could ever share. It's a message that applies to believers and non-believers alike.

All people, long-time Christians included, can be caught up in all kinds of sin. Sometimes it's easy to fall into thinking that it's OK to keep on sinning since we know that Jesus will forgive us of our sins when we ask Him. While that's true, it's also equally true that He calls us to repent of our sins. While Jesus' death spares us from the eternal consequences of our sins, He also wants to spare us from the earthly consequences of our sins.

Every sin we commit takes one more notch out of our lives. Sin destroys our relationships with God and with others. Sin keeps us from seeing clearly, acting appropriately, and experiencing the abundant life that God wants us to live.

If we want to love others like Jesus loved them, it seems that we need to be willing to preach to others like Jesus preached to them. We don't have to preach in a way that is "holier than thou," and God wants us to be wise about where, when, and with whom we share any words from Him. But if we want to have true concern for others, one of the best ways to show them that we really care for them, and love them, is to share the message of repentance with them.

The book of James is one of the most compassionate books in the whole Bible, calling believers to put their faith into action on behalf of others. In addition to calling us to do things like feed and clothe those in need, James ends his book with these words:

"My brothers, if one of you should wander from the

truth and someone should bring him back, remember this: whoever turns a sinner from the error of his way will save him from death and cover over a multitude of sins" (James 5:19-20).

The next time I'm afraid to approach someone regarding their sins, I need to remember that this is one of the most loving things I could ever do for them. If I want to truly walk as Jesus walked, I need to be willing to preach as Jesus preached. In doing so, I may be able to "save them from death and cover over a multitude of sins."

PRAYER: FATHER, HELP ME BE WILLING TO PREACH THE MESSAGE OF REPENTANCE WHERE, WHEN, AND TO WHOM YOU CALL ME TO PREACH IT, AS A WAY OF TRULY EXPRESSING YOUR LOVE TOWARDS THEM. IN JESUS' NAME, AMEN.

Lesson 5

GETTING TO THE
HEART OF LOVE

Scripture Reading: Matthew 5

I tried pole vaulting back when I was in Junior High. The goal was to take a long pole in your hands, then run with all your might and plant the end of the pole in a box just in front of a bar raised high on two other bars in front of you. All I remember was that when I tried it, I felt an incredible jolt when I planted the pole in the box. Not only did I not make it over the bar, I didn't even make it off the ground!

I've since learned that part of the trick is getting the pole to bend properly. As the pole bends, it transfers all of the energy of the runner into the pole, which then helps to propel the runner up and over the bar at the top.

I bring this up because I sometimes feel the same kind of jolt when I read Jesus' words in Matthew chapter 5 about how to love others. I want to love others, and I think I'm a loving person much of the time, but as I read what true love really involves, not only do I not think I'm making it over the bar, I'm not even sure I'm making it off the ground.

The reason I feel this way is because Jesus gets to the heart of love in this passage. Rather than lowering the bar for all of us, Jesus raises it...or more accurately, He shows us what's really involved in loving others.

He gives several examples:

- *"You have heard that it was said to the people long ago, 'Do not murder, and anyone who murders will be subject to judgment.' But I tell you that anyone who is angry with his brother will be subject to judgment" (Matthew 5:21-22).*
- *"You have heard that it was said, 'Do not commit adultery.' But I tell you that anyone who looks at a woman lustfully has already committed adultery with her in his heart" (Matthew 5:27-28).*
- *"Again, you have heard that it was said to the people long ago, 'Do not break your oath, but keep the oaths you have made to the Lord.' But I tell you, Do not swear at all...Simply let your 'Yes' be 'Yes,' and your 'No,' 'No'; any-*

thing beyond this comes from the evil one"
(Matthew 5:33-34, 37).

Then He concludes with these astounding words:

"You have heard that it was said, 'Love your neighbor and hate your enemy.' But I tell you: Love your enemies and pray for those who persecute you, that you may be sons of your Father in heaven. He causes his sun to rise on the evil and the good, and sends rain on the righteous and the unrighteous. If you love those who love you, what reward will you get? Are not even the tax collectors doing that? And if you greet only your brothers, what are you doing more than others? Do not even pagans do that? Be perfect, therefore, as your heavenly Father is perfect" (Matthew 5:43-48).

Talk about raising the bar! It's hard enough to be consistent in loving my wife, my family, and my friends. But to love my enemies, too? That's impossible! Or at least it would be without Christ.

When we let the love of Christ flow through us to others, all things are possible. He's able to transfer all of His energy and love into us, and then propel us over even the highest bar. And you know what? When we're able to get our hearts right and let Christ work through us to love even our enemies, imagine what kind of love we could show to those who already love us!

Rather than giving us an impossible task, Jesus shows us that true love comes from Him, then flows out to others. Let His love flow through you today.

PRAYER: FATHER, POUR OUT YOUR LOVE INTO MY HEART AGAIN TODAY SO THAT I CAN LOVE OTHERS THE WAY YOU WANT ME TO...EVEN MY ENEMIES. IN JESUS' NAME, AMEN.

Doing A
Heart Check

Scripture Reading: Matthew 6

There are times when we need to show people that we love them. It's important that we let them know, in tangible ways, that we appreciate them, care for them, and are willing to do anything for them.

I remember talking to a husband who was about to get a divorce from his wife because she wanted them to move across the country, but he didn't want to. I asked him: "If someone were threatening your wife's life, would you be willing to die for her?" "Yes," he answered, "I would." So I added, "If you're willing to die for her, would you be willing to live for her?" He recommitted his life to Christ and to his marriage and they were soon reconciled to each each other.

This kind of tangible expression of our love can make or break a relationship.

But there are other times when God calls us to do our acts of love in secret, in ways that only God Himself can see. Jesus tells us the reason why in Matthew chapter 6:

> *"Be careful not to do your 'acts of righteousness' before men, to be seen by them. If you do, you will have no reward from your Father in heaven. So when you give to the needy, do not announce it with trumpets, as the hypocrites do in the synagogues and on the streets, to be honored by men. I tell you the truth, they have received their reward in full. But when you give to the needy, do not let your left hand know what your right hand is doing, so that your giving may be in secret. Then your Father, who sees what is done in secret, will reward you"* (Matthew 6:1-4).

This passage serves as a "heart-check" for me. When I'm considering doing some "acts of righteousness," or "acts of love," I always want to check my motives. Am I wanting to do these things out of an attempt to love others more? Or out of an attempt to get others to love me more? These are two very different things.

To reiterate this thought, Jesus gives us a second example that applies when we pray for others:

"And when you pray, do not be like the hypocrites, for they love to pray standing in the synagogues and on the street corners to be seen by men. I tell you the truth, they have received their reward in full. But when you pray, go into your room, close the door and pray to your Father, who is unseen. Then your Father, who sees what is done in secret, will reward you" (Matthew 6:5-6).

As if to underscore it one more time, Jesus gives us a third example, too:

"When you fast, do not look somber as the hypocrites do, for they disfigure their faces to show men they are fasting. I tell you the truth, they have received their reward in full. But when you fast, put oil on your head and wash your face, so that it will not be obvious to men that you are fasting, but only to your Father, who is unseen; and your Father, who sees what is done in secret, will reward you" (Matthew 6:16-18).

Each of these examples remind me that there are times when our giving, our praying, and our fasting are to be done in secret, with no thought of the fact that others may never know who gave to them, prayed for them, or fasted on behalf of them. These are good reminders to me to check my heart even when I feel prompted to express my love in a more visible way. I need to always be sure that my motivation is to truly show others how much I love them, rather than trying to get them to love me more.

God promises that He will not leave our good deeds unrewarded, but by promising to reward us Himself, it frees us from trying to get our rewards from those we're trying to love. It's this kind of heart-check that will help us to truly love others more.

PRAYER: FATHER, HELP ME TO KEEP MY HEART IN CHECK, SO THAT I CAN TRULY EXPRESS MY LOVE FOR OTHERS IN WAYS THAT TRULY BLESSES THEIR LIVES. IN JESUS' NAME, AMEN.

Lesson 7

GOLDEN
LOVE

Scripture Reading: Matthew 7

One year ago this weekend, I was headed to the African country of Swaziland. Eighty of us from the U.S. were on a missions trip to work side-by-side with the people of Swaziland to plant thousands of vegetable gardens near their homes.

On the trip, I met a man who helped me see what it takes to live a life of sacrificial love. He was a pastor who had worked with this organization for over a year, helping to plant gardens throughout the country with dozens of teams that had come over to help.

One day, I was looking at a map of Swaziland with him. The map showed which areas of the country had already been planted, and which areas still needed to be planted. We were planting in one of the last areas remaining in the country, but I noticed there was still one more area yet to be planted. I asked him about it, and he said that the one remaining area was the village where he lived.

I couldn't believe it. I turned and looked at him and said, "You've been bringing teams over here, helping people plant all over the country, but you haven't brought a team to help you plant in your own village yet?"

He replied, "We have a saying here in Swaziland: 'We would rather starve than let our guests go hungry.' " He went on to explain: he wanted to make sure that all of the other areas were served first, then he would bring a team to his own area. I about burst into tears on the spot. It still makes my eyes water just thinking about it.

There's a verse of scripture in the middle of Matthew chapter 7 that people refer to as "The Golden Rule." (And it's not, "He who has the gold makes the rules"!) Jesus included these words in his sermon on the mount, saying that they sum up the teachings that God had given up to that point:

"So in everything, do to others what you would have them do to you, for this sums up the Law and the Prophets" (Matthew 7:12).

Do to others what you would have them
do to you. It seems like such a simple
thing...and sometimes it is. If a storeowner
gives you too much change at the store, you
can hand back the extra change, because that's
what you would want a customer to do if they
came into your store. Or if you notice someone who needs money for a worthy project,
you might give it to them because you know
that if you needed money for a worthy
project, you'd want them to help you.

But sometimes it's a much harder thing to
do. Sometimes, as in the case of this pastor
from Swaziland, allowing others to go ahead
of you can literally mean death for someone
you love.

How can anyone live that kind of life?
How can anyone have that much love for others, that they would let someone in their own
family perish so that someone else might live?

How? God gave us the ultimate example
of just such a love when He allowed His own
Son, Jesus, to die in our place. When Jesus
called us to "do to others what you would
have them do to you," He was calling us to do
something that He Himself would soon be

doing to the fullest extent, giving of His own life so that we could live.

Last time I mentioned that God wants us to be willing to live for others. This time, the call is to be willing to die for them, too. Jesus calls us to be willing to do both. When our hearts are at that point of willingness, we'll know that we have achieved the greatest love possible.

We'll have a love like that of Christ Himself who said, and then later exemplified for us, these words:

"Greater love has no one than this, that he lay down his life for his friends" (John 15:13).

PRAYER: FATHER, HELP ME TO DO FOR OTHERS AS I WOULD HAVE THEM DO FOR ME. IN JESUS' NAME, AMEN.

Lesson 8

LOVE
THAT HEALS

Scripture Reading: Matthew 8

Do you know someone who's sick? I'd like to encourage you to pray for them.

Our prayers do make a difference. When Jesus walked the earth, He was moved with compassion for those around Him, healing those who needed healing. If we want to express the love of Christ like He did, one of the things we can do is to try to alleviate the pain and suffering of those we come in contact with, too.

Take a look at what Jesus did for three people in Matthew chapter 8 who were sick:

First, there's the man with leprosy who came to Jesus and said,

"Lord, if You are willing, You can make me clean." Jesus reached out His hand and touched the man. "I am willing," He said, "Be clean!"

Immediately he was cured of his leprosy (Matthew 8:2-3).

Second, there's the army officer who came to Jesus asking for help.

"Lord," he said, "my servant lies at home paralyzed and in terrible suffering."
Jesus said to him, "I will go and heal him" (Matthew 8:5-7)

When the officer protests Jesus' offer to come to his house in person because he feels he doesn't deserve to have Jesus come under his roof, Jesus sees the officers' faith and declares:

"Go! It will be done just as you believed it would"
And his servant was healed at that very hour (Matthew 8:13).

Third, there's Peter's mother-in-law, lying in bed with a fever. When Jesus came into Peter's house, Jesus saw her, touched her hand, and the fever left her. She got up and began to wait on Jesus (see Matthew 8:14-15).

These are just a few of the many acts of

healing that Jesus did for those around Him. While there are many more recorded in the Bible, these are enough for me today to recognize that one of the ways we can express love to others is through healing.

I don't know what you've experienced when you've prayed for people to be healed. I've prayed for people who have been surprisingly healed, and I've prayed for others who have unfortunately died. But I come back to the fact that God is a healing God, and that Jesus regularly and consistently healed those He came in contact with. So I've continued to regularly and consistently pray for those around me to be healed, and I've seen people healed time after time.

I also take encouragement from all of the prayers that have gone before me for diseases that were once thought to be fatal and incurable. I think about diseases that here in the U.S. were once devastating, like polio, which in 1952 was out of control, crippling 21,000 people a year, mostly children, and killing 3,100. Then came doctors Salk and Sabin who searched for a solution to this epidemic and found them by producing the injectable and oral polio vaccines.

Whenever I pray for people with cancer, or other fatal, crippling or incurable diseases, I also pray that God will reveal the cure to someone, to some researcher, or even to me or to my children. God has answered such prayers in the past, and God will answer such prayers in the future. Our prayers are never in vain, when we put our faith in the God who heals, and put our trust in Him with the timing and the outcome.

Pray for those around you to be healed. Type out your prayers in an email to them. Give them a call and pray for them over the phone. Take a cue from Jesus: when someone stops to tell you about their sickness, take a minute right then and there to pray for them.

There's no doubt when I read the Scriptures that one of the ways that Jesus expressed His love to others was through healing. Maybe that's a way you can express your love to others, too.

PRAYER: FATHER, HELP ME TO PRAY FOR THOSE WHO ARE SICK, AND TO KEEP PRAYING FOR THEM, THAT THEY WOULD BE HEALED IN JESUS' NAME, AMEN.

BRING YOUR FRIENDS TO JESUS

Scripture Reading: Matthew 9

Do you have some friends who could use a touch from Jesus? I'd like to encourage you to bring them to Him today.

Whether they need healing, a change of heart, a change of lifestyle, or a change in their eternal destination, Jesus can do it. I know, because He did it for me when I was reading Matthew chapter 9, twenty years ago. Now I want to bring as many people as I can to Jesus so He can do the same things for them.

Look with me at what Jesus did in Matthew chapter 9 when some people brought their friends and family members to Jesus:

First, we have the men who brought their paralyzed friend, lying on a mat, to be healed by Jesus. The Bible says that "when Jesus saw their faith," He healed the paralytic and forgave him of his sins. The man took up his mat and went home, and the crowd was filled with awe and praised God (see Matthew 9:1-8). Note what it was that triggered Jesus' action in this passage: it says that He did these things for the paralytic "when Jesus saw THEIR faith."

Next, we have Matthew, the author of this book of the Bible, who had Jesus over to his house for dinner. It seems that Matthew also invited many of his fellow tax collectors and other "sinners" to eat with him and Jesus and the disciples. Even though Jesus was criticized by some people for going to the house of someone like Matthew, Jesus made it clear that these were exactly the people He came for. In response to these critics, Jesus said, "It is not the healthy who need a doctor, but the sick...For I have not come to call the righteous, but sinners" (see Matthew 9:9-13). Jesus wants us to invite Him over to meet our unsaved, and perhaps unwholesome, friends!

Third, we have the father, Jairus, who couldn't bring his dying daughter to Jesus, so Jairus brought Jesus to her. When Jesus got to his house, the girl had already died. Those in the house told Jairus, "Your daughter is dead. Why bother the teacher [Jesus] any more?" Ignoring what they said, Jesus told Jairus, "Don't be afraid; just believe." Then Jesus walked into the house, took the girl by the hand and said, "Little girl, I say to you, get up!" Immediately she got up and walked around (see Matthew 9:18-26 and Mark 5:22-43). Even though the girl wasn't able to come to Jesus herself, her father was still able to bring Jesus to her.

Do you see the influence each of these people had on their friends and family? By bringing their friends and family to Jesus, or bringing Jesus to them, their friends and family were healed, changed, forgiven and given a new life! How would you like to be used by God like that? You can! Even today, this week, this month!

Bring your friends to Jesus, or bring Jesus to them. With Easter just around the corner, you've got a perfect opportunity to invite your unchurched friends to church. This is a time when they may be most likely to attend, if at all. It's a time when they can hear the story of the resurrection, and begin their journey with the Living God.

One of the people who played a crucial role in my own salvation was my cousin who invited me to her church when I moved to her city. Within a year of attending her church, I put my faith in Christ.

Maybe that's what God wants to do through you, too? He's looking for people to join Him in His work. As Jesus said at the end of this chapter:

> *"The harvest is plentiful but the workers are few. Ask the Lord of the harvest, therefore, to send out workers into his harvest field"* (Matthew 9:37-38).

Want to be one of those workers? Bring your friends to Jesus!

PRAYER: FATHER, HELP ME HAVE THE COURAGE TO STEP OUT AND BRING MY FRIENDS TO JESUS, SO HE CAN TOUCH THEIR LIVES AS HE'S TOUCHED MINE. IN JESUS' NAME, AMEN.

Lesson 10

PERFECT LOVE
DRIVES OUT FEAR

Scripture Reading: Matthew 10

I had a chance to go to Israel in 1995 and stand in front of a cross that many believe marks the spot where Jesus died. As I stood on that hallowed spot, I couldn't help but drop to my knees and say, "Thank You!" over and over for what Jesus had done for me.

When I finally stood up, I walked back across the room to talk to the man who had brought me to this place. Although he was my host for the week, he wasn't a believer. In fact, he had made it quite clear that he was opposed to the gospel of Jesus Christ, and to Christianity as a whole.

But as I returned to him from the foot of the cross, I couldn't help but tell him why I had dropped to my knees. I couldn't help but tell him about this Man, Jesus, who loved me so much that He was willing to die in my place for the sins that I had committed. I couldn't help but tell him that I was alive because Jesus died.

I was so overwhelmed with God's love that it drove out my fear.

There's a passage in Matthew 10 where Jesus tells his disciples to go into the surrounding communities and preach about the kingdom of heaven, heal the sick, raise the dead, and drive out demons. Jesus told them that even though He was sending them out like sheep among wolves, that they didn't have to be afraid:

> *"Do not be afraid of those who kill the body but cannot kill the soul. Rather, be afraid of the One who can destroy both soul and body in hell. Are not two sparrows sold for a penny? Yet not one of them will fall to the ground apart from the will of your Father. And even the very hairs of your head are all numbered. So don't be afraid; you are worth more than many sparrows"* *(Matthew 10:28-31).*

I remember many times during my trip when fear crept up on me. I remember walking down a long corridor in an airport in Germany, late at night and all alone, to board the plane to Israel. At the end of the corridor was a guard behind a bulletproof glass with a gun pointed at me through a tiny hole. I began to question why I had come when the words from a Veggietales video came to mind. I began to sing under my breath, "God is bigger than the boogie man...He's bigger than Godzilla and the monsters on TV..." God filled me with His peace.

I remember being afraid when I pulled up to the house where I was going to stay. The people I was going to stay with were relatives of someone I knew here in the States, but I knew they might be openly hostile to Christ. A wave of fear passed through me as I stepped out of the car to greet the eldest member of this extended family. In that moment, God reminded me of some verses from the Bible:

"When you enter a house, first say, 'Peace to this house.' If a man of peace is there, your peace will rest on him; if not, it will return to you. Stay in that house, eating and drinking whatever they give you... Do not move around from house to house" *(Luke 10:5-7).*

I happened to remember the traditional greeting meant "Peace be with you," so I put out my hand and said, "Salam aleikum." I didn't know what he might do. He took hold of my hand and shook it firmly, saying, "wa-aleikum-as-salam," which means, "and peace be with you." I was suddenly at peace again and knew that I was right where God wanted me to be.

Jesus said, "perfect love drives out fear" (1 John 4:18). Call on God's perfect love to fill you today. As He does, boldly share the love that He's poured out on you with others.

PRAYER: FATHER, FILL ME WITH YOUR PERFECT LOVE THAT DRIVES OUT FEAR, SO THAT I CAN BOLDLY SHARE ABOUT CHRIST WITH THOSE I LOVE. IN JESUS' NAME, AMEN.

Lesson 11

Loving Others Through Their Doubts

Scripture Reading: Matthew 11

What do you do when someone you love begins to have doubts about God? Or when they've never put their faith in Him at all? One of the best things you can do is to love them through their doubts.

Take a look at how Jesus did this in Matthew chapter 11. In this chapter, Jesus actually deals with three different categories of doubters, using three different approaches.

The first category is made up of what I would call "honest doubters" -- people who want to believe, but because of circumstances or sincere challenges to their faith, they're looking for answers to help them overcome their unbelief.

As surprising as it may seem, John the Baptist may have been one of these men. Even though John is the one who baptized Jesus, who proclaimed, "Look, the Lamb of God, who takes away the sin of the world!" (John 1:29b), when John landed in prison, he sent disciples to ask Jesus, "Are you the one who was to come, or should we expect someone else?" (Matthew 11:3).

Jesus didn't rebuke John for the question, but instead simply said,

> *"Go back and report to John what you hear and see: The blind receive sight, the lame walk, those who have leprosy are cured, the deaf hear, the dead are raised, and the good news is preached to the poor" (Matthew 11:4-5).*

Then Jesus commends John to the listening crowd:

> *"Among those born of women there has not risen anyone greater than John the Baptist" (Matthew 11:11).*

Sometimes people need a gentle reminder of all that Christ has done, and continues to do, even if they aren't seeing it right then in their own life.

The second category is made of up what I would call "skeptical doubters" -- people who stand back and cross their arms while they look at the facts, seeing if they line up with their preconceived notions of what a man of God should or should not do. In their attempts to be "wise," they can sometimes shut out the possibility of faith because Jesus doesn't meet their expectations.

Jesus pointed out the dilemma of such expectations by saying,

> *"John came neither eating nor drinking, and they say, 'He has a demon.' The Son of Man [Jesus] came eating and drinking, and they say, 'Here is a glutton and a drunkard, a friend of tax collectors and 'sinners.' But wisdom is proved right by her actions"* *(Matthew 11:18-19).*

Sometimes people need to hear a wise response that challenges their assumptions and gives them true wisdom so they can put their faith in Christ.

The third category is made up of what I would call "stubborn doubters" -- people who don't want to believe regardless of the evidence. Jesus sharply rebukes those who lived in the cities where He performed most of His miracles by saying,

"Woe to you, Korazin! Woe to you, Bethsaida! If the miracles that were performed in you had been performed in Tyre and Sidon, they would have repented long ago in sackcloth and ashes." (Matthew 11: 21-22).

But even in this sharp rebuke, I don't think Jesus was wasting His breath. Sometimes people need a strong wake-up call to get them thinking clearly again and respond in faith.

The best way to help people who have doubts is to love them through it, whether that love takes the form of a gentle reminder, a wise response, or a sharp rebuke.

Jesus concludes by calling us all to put our complete trust in Him:

"Come to me, all you who are weary and burdened, and I will give you rest. Take my yoke upon you and learn from me, for I am gentle and humble in heart, and you will find rest for your souls. For my yoke is easy and my burden is light" (Matthew 11:28-30).

Jesus wants you to come to Him today,

putting your complete trust in Him, and encouraging others to do the same.

PRAYER: FATHER, I'M GOING TO PUT MY COMPLETE TRUST IN YOU TODAY, AND I ASK THAT YOU WOULD HELP TO TO ENCOURAGE OTHERS TO DO THE SAME. IN JESUS' NAME, AMEN.

Lesson 12

LOVE DOES
WHAT'S RIGHT

Scripture Reading: Matthew 12

Bow many times have you pulled back from loving others because doing so might bring on some unwanted consequences? Is it OK to pull back sometimes because of the threats? Or should we always press ahead regardless of the threats?

These are questions Jesus faced on a regular basis. And it's encouraging to me to see that He handled different situations differently.

Let's look at just two of these situations from Matthew 12. The first deals with whether or not Jesus would heal a man, even though doing so might cost Jesus His life.

> *"Going on from that place, He went into their synagogue, and a man with a shriveled hand was there. Looking for a reason to accuse Jesus, they asked Him, 'Is it lawful to heal on the Sabbath?' He said to them, 'If any of you has a sheep and it*

falls into a pit on the Sabbath, will you not take hold of it and lift it out? How much more valuable is a man than a sheep! Therefore it is lawful to do good on the Sabbath.' Then He said to the man, 'Stretch out your hand.' So he stretched it out and it was completely restored, just as sound as the other. But the Pharisees went out and plotted how they might kill Jesus" (Matthew 12:9-14).

Jesus was facing a setup, and He could have backed away because of the threat. But rather than backing down, and leaving the man's hand shriveled, Jesus put His love for the man ahead of His own life. He did what was right, even when threatened. That's a bold kind of love.

But in the next situation, Jesus takes a different approach:

"Aware of this, Jesus withdrew from that place. Many followed Him, and He healed all their sick, warning them not to tell who He was" (Matthew 12:15).

Matthew says this was to fulfill what the prophet Isaiah said:

"He will not quarrel or cry out; no one will hear His voice in the streets. A bruised reed He will not break, and a smoldering wick He will not snuff out, till He leads justice to victory" (Matthew 12:19-20).

Jesus could have backed off at this point, and stopped healing people all together. But instead, He continued to heal many, even though it was no longer in the open, and even with a warning telling people not to tell others who He was. He showed the same bold love, but with a different approach.

There are times when we need to openly challenge irrational thinking. But there are other times when we need to simply do what's right in quiet. In either case, the bottom line is still this: to continue loving others and doing what God has called us to do, rather than backing off because of people's threats.

I faced a dilemma one day when I was asked to lead worship at our church. In putting together the set of songs for that morning, one song stood out in my mind above all the others. I knew it would be the song where people would really meet God in the worship time. But the very next day, I got a note from someone who for some reason felt compelled to tell me there was one song we should never sing in church. It was the very song I planned to do, but hadn't even told anyone I was doing!

It wasn't a life-threatening dilemma, but it was a real one. Would I continue with the worship set as I had planned, knowing how powerful it could be? Or would I back down and try to please this person? I decided to do the song, and it was powerful.

We all face similar dilemmas every day. Will we give up because of someone's threats? Or will be go forth and do what's right, trusting God to work out the details? In all cases, I pray we will always put love first, not the threats.

PRAYER: FATHER, HELP ME TO ALWAYS MOVE FORWARD IN LOVE, DOING WHAT'S RIGHT, EVEN WHEN THREATENED. IN JESUS' NAME, AMEN.

LOVING OTHERS THROUGH PARABLES

Scripture Reading: Matthew 13

The sun and the wind decided to have a contest one day to see which of them was the strongest. When they saw a man walking down the street wearing a warm winter coat, they agreed that whoever could get the man's coat off would truly be the strongest.

The wind thought this would be a piece of cake, so he began to blow with all his might. But the harder he blew, the tighter the man held onto his coat. Eventually, the wind gave up, and the sun took a turn. The sun came out from behind a cloud and began to shine brighter and brighter. As the man got hotter and hotter, he finally took off the coat of his own accord. The wind had to concede that the sun was indeed stronger.

When trying to get your family and friends to put their faith more fully in God, which approach do you think would work best? To blow harder and harder like the wind, or to shine brighter and brighter like the sun?

I had to use this illustration one day to help a friend. Although he meant well, his actions toward others often had the effect of repelling them from what he wanted them to do, rather than drawing them to do it of their own accord. I could have just told him directly what was happening, but I felt by using a parable, he might be able to see better what was really happening.

Jesus knew the power of parables, too, telling them often. Matthew includes seven of Jesus' parables in Matthew chapter 13: the parables of the sower, the weeds, the mustard seed, the yeast, the hidden treasure, the pearl, and the net. Matthew says:

"Jesus spoke all these things to the crowd in parables; he did not say anything to them without using a parable" (Matthew 13:34).

Why did Jesus use so many parables? When asked this question by His disciples, Jesus replied, in part: "Though seeing, they do not see; though hearing, they do not hear or understand" (Matthew 13:13). When confronted directly, people's defensiveness can sometimes cloud their thinking to words that could otherwise be truly helpful. People can often see a point better when it is illustrated as an external reality first, then they can apply the principle to their own lives internally.

The prophet Nathan used this approach when speaking to King David when David committed adultery with another man's wife. Nathan said:

> *"There were two men in a certain town, one rich and the other poor. The rich man had a very large number of sheep and cattle, but the poor man had nothing except one little ewe lamb he had bought. He raised it, and it grew up with him and his children. It shared his food, drank from his cup and even slept in his arms. It was like a daughter to him.*
>
> *"Now a traveler came to the rich man, but the rich man refrained from taking one of his own sheep or cattle to prepare a meal for the traveler who had come to him. Instead, he took the ewe lamb that belonged to the poor man and prepared it for the one who had come to him."*
>
> *David burned with anger against the man and said to Nathan, "As surely as the LORD lives, the*

man who did this deserves to die! He must pay for
that lamb four times over, because he did such a
thing and had no pity."
Then Nathan said to David, "You are the man!"
(2 Samuel 12:1b-7a).

Through this story, David was finally able
to see the truth of what he had done, leading
him to true repentance.

The next time you have to approach someone with something that might be hard to
share directly, try using a parable, an illustration or a story. Rather than blowing harder
and harder like the wind, try shining brighter
and brighter like the sun!

PRAYER: FATHER, GIVE ME WISDOM TO KNOW HOW
TO APPROACH THOSE I LOVE, SO THAT THEY MAY
HEAR YOUR TRUTH IN A WAY THAT MOVES THEM TO
ACTION. IN JESUS' NAME, AMEN.

BALANCING LOVING ACTIONS WITH LOVING PRAYERS

Scripture Reading: Matthew 14

How do you balance the time you spend loving others with your actions and taking time alone to pray? How do you meet the needs of others and still have time alone with God? One way is to follow the example of Jesus in Matthew chapter 14. Although Jesus was regularly among the multitudes, He also regularly withdrew to solitary places to pray.

In this passage, Jesus and His disciples were inundated with people who needed them. In fact, Mark says that "so many people were coming and going that they did not even have a chance to eat," so Jesus said to the disciples,

> *"Come with me by yourselves to a quiet place and get some rest" (Mark 6:31).*

It was also at this time that Jesus truly

needed some time alone with His Father. John the Baptist had just been beheaded -- John, who was Jesus' cousin, Jesus' baptizer, Jesus' forerunner in calling the people to repentance, and Jesus' predecessor in giving his life for the kingdom of God.

But as Jesus tried to withdraw to a quiet place, the inevitable happened. When His boat landed, the people had already beaten him to the spot on foot. Mark says,

"When Jesus landed and saw a large crowd, he had compassion on them, because they were like sheep without a shepherd. So he began teaching them many things" (Mark 6:33).

It was in this context that Jesus performed one of his most famous miracles. It had been a long day of ministering to the people and the disciples finally said to Jesus,

"Send the crowds away, so they can go to the villages and buy themselves some food" (Matthew 14:15b).

I can almost read their thoughts between the lines: "and maybe we'll finally get a chance to eat, too!" That's why they came out to this solitary area in the first place!

There were over 5,000 people there, and all the disciples could find were five loaves of bread and two fish. Jesus looked to heaven, gave thanks, the food turned out to be enough for everyone, with twelve basketfuls left over...one for each of the disciples!

Now fast forward a few hours, and we find that Jesus was finally able to get alone to pray. He sent the crowds home satisfied, and sent the disciples on ahead by boat to their next stop. After praying, Jesus was able to perform another of his most famous miracles: He walked across the water to rejoin them in the boat.

It's interesting to me that two of Jesus' most famous miracles were done for the sake of expediency, not for the sake of wowing the people! While Jesus obviously made it a priority to be with people and love them as much as possible, He also made it a priority to take time alone to pray. Through those prayers, God was able to accomplish things that would otherwise have been humanly impossible.

Elijah did some of his most impressive

miracles for the sake of expediency, too, such as splitting a river in two so he could cross over on dry ground. He didn't do this to impress anyone; he simply had places to go and people to see before he was taken to heaven (see 2 Kings, chapter 2).

Has God given you seemingly impossible tasks? Do the needs around you overwhelm your human abilities to meet them? Let me encourage you to take time alone to pray. I've heard several spiritual men and women say, "I have so much to do, I don't have time NOT to pray." They realize that it is only through prayer that they will be able to accomplish all that God has put on their hearts to do.

No matter what else you have to do today, make sure you take time to pray.

Get alone with God, the Creator of time itself. He'll show you how to make the most of the time He's given you, even accomplishing things that seem humanly impossible!

PRAYER: FATHER, GIVE ME SUPERNATURAL WISDOM TO KNOW HOW TO DO ALL THAT YOU'VE PUT ON MY HEART TO DO. IN JESUS' NAME, AMEN.

Lesson 15

LOVING OTHERS WITH PERSISTENT FAITH

Scripture Reading: Matthew 15

Have you ever felt like God is ignoring your prayers? Or when you share your hopes with others, they tell you not to bother God with the request? Or when God does answer, it's not really the answer you're looking for?

Or possibly worst of all, have you ever poured out your heart's desire, only to be rebuked so sharply that you wished you had never asked at all?

If so, I want to encourage you not to give up on your prayers too quickly. God may still have something in store for you.

Take a look at a real live woman who came to Jesus with a request in Matthew chapter 15.

This woman must have heard or seen some of the miracles that Jesus had done, for she came pleading to Him to heal her daughter.

She cried out, "Lord, Son of David, have mercy on

me! My daughter is suffering terribly from demon-possession."

But look at what Jesus did next. The Bible says, "Jesus did not answer a word." Wow! Not a word! This is pretty shocking, considering all that Jesus did for so many people. Yet it looked like He was just going to ignore the woman completely. But as shocking as that was, look at what Jesus' disciples did next. The Bible says,

"So his disciples came to him and urged him, 'Send her away, for she keeps crying out after us.' "

Wow! As if it weren't bad enough to be ignored, the ones who claimed to be followers of Jesus came and told her to get lost, too.

So Jesus finally breaks His silence. But when He does speak, it's hardly the answer the woman was looking for. Jesus says,

"I was sent only to the lost sheep of Israel."

She was a Canaanite, not a Jew, not one of the "lost sheep of Israel." What? Jesus, of all people? Not being willing to help someone, regardless of who they were?

Imagine the thoughts that could have gone through her mind, thoughts that might go through our minds too if we were in her situation: "I should have known better. I don't know why I thought Jesus would ever want to help someone like me. I'm sure He does love some people, but probably not people like me." Had the woman given up there, the story might have ended very differently. But she didn't. She persisted in her faith. She came to Jesus and knelt before Him:

"Lord, help me!" she said.

Then came what could have been the worst blow of all: Jesus replied,

"It is not right to take the children's bread and toss it to their dogs."

I don't know if Jesus was just testing her faith here, or trying to teach something to the disciples, but whatever the reason, she may have been wishing by this point that she had never asked at all.

But she didn't. She had a daughter that she loved, a daughter that desperately needed healing. She tossed aside whatever feelings she may have had, and held firm in her faith. She knew she could trust Jesus' heart. She knew she could trust His character. She knew she could trust Jesus to do what's best.

She replied: "Yes, Lord, but even the dogs eat the crumbs that fall from their masters' table."

And Jesus honored her persistent faith. He answered,

"Woman, you have great faith! Your request is granted." And her daughter was healed from that very hour.

Jesus is trustworthy, even when He's silent. Jesus is trustworthy, even when others may tell you to go away. Jesus is trustworthy, even when you may not like the answers. Jesus is trustworthy, even when your hopes are dashed and you wonder if you should have ever asked at all.

Persist in your faith, especially on behalf of those you love. As you do, I pray that you'll eventually hear Jesus say to you, too: "You have great faith! Your request is granted."

PRAYER: FATHER, INCREASE MY FAITH SO THAT IT PERSISTS EVEN IN THE FACE OF SILENCE, FRUSTRATION OR DISCOURAGEMENT, ALL SO THAT I CAN SEE YOUR WILL DONE HERE ON EARTH. IN JESUS' NAME, AMEN.

Lesson 16

Loving Others By Dying To Self

Scripture Reading: Matthew 16

A friend was praying with me one day when she said something so profound I wrote it down. I didn't even fully understand what she was saying at the time, and I'm not sure I completely understand it still! But I knew that what she said contained a truth that I needed to hear and explore. She said:

> *"Beware of unbroken men, and beware of unbrokenness in yourself."*

She was concerned that there may be people who would want to exploit some of my gifts that God had given me for their own purposes, rather than His purposes. And she was concerned that because of my own wants and needs and desires, that I might be swayed to believe and follow those who wanted to put my gifts to use.

I understood the concern, but I still had a lot of questions. What is an "unbroken man"? What does "unbrokenness" look like? How should I respond when presented with various opportunities to use my gifts?

There's a passage in Matthew 16 that sheds some light on this for me. It begins with Jesus warning the disciples:

> *"Be on your guard against the yeast of the Pharisees and Sadducees" (Matthew 16:5b).*

Jesus goes on to explain this in a way that the disciples could understand that they were to beware of the teaching of the Pharisees and Sadducees, the religious leaders of the day.

While the Pharisees and Sadducees claimed to follow the teachings of God, and may have at times been sincerely trying to follow Him, they often succumbed to protecting themselves and their traditions rather than giving their lives truly for others. In a sense, they were still "unbroken men," men who still seemed to "have it together" and were trying desperately to "keep it together," when in reality, they would have been better off realizing that they didn't have it together at all, and it was only God who could hold them together.

But within the very same passage, Jesus shows that it wasn't only the Pharisees and Saducees that the disciples needed to be on guard against, but themselves as well, their own thoughts and desires. Jesus shows how quickly we can go from following God's thoughts and desires to following our own when He asks the disciples who they think He is.

Simon Peter answered: *"You are the Christ, the Son of the living God" (Matthew 16:16).* Jesus commends Peter by saying, *"Blessed are you, Simon son of Jonah, for this was not revealed to you by man, but by my Father in heaven,"* and then by describing the powerful role Peter will play in building God's kingdom on earth and in heaven.

But in the very next passage, as Jesus explains that He will soon suffer, die and be raised to life again, Peter exclaims: *"Never Lord! This shall never happen to you!"* Look at what Jesus says to Peter this time:

"Jesus turned and said to Peter, 'Get behind me, Satan! You are a stumbling block to me; you do

not have in mind the things of God, but the things of men."' (Matthew 16:23).

Within a span of only a few minutes, Peter went from being commended for expressing a truth that he had received from God, to being condemned for expressing a falsehood that came from his own thinking.

How can we guard against "unbrokenness," against harmful thoughts and teachings, whether in others or in ourselves? Jesus tells us one way in the next sentence:

"Then Jesus said to his disciples, 'If anyone would come after me, he must deny himself and take up his cross and follow me. For whoever wants to save his life will lose it, but whoever loses his life for me will find it'" (Matthew 16:24-25).

If our thinking is based on trying to save ourselves, protect ourselves, defend ourselves, it may be our undoing. While it's not always wrong to save, protect and defend ourselves, it is if it keeps us from doing what's right.

Instead of trying to "keep it together," my prayer is to realize how truly broken I am. In the end, it's by putting my full faith and trust in God that I will truly be able to "keep it together."

PRAYER: FATHER, HELP ME TO TRUST YOU FULLY, SO THAT I CAN LOVE OTHERS FULLY, WITHOUT REGARD FOR MY OWN LIFE. IN JESUS' NAME, AMEN.

Lesson 17

LOVING OTHERS BY INCREASING OUR FAITH

Scripture Reading: Matthew 17

I've mentioned before how our faith can affect those we love. Today I'd like to talk about increasing our faith, so we can affect others even more.

Take a look at the example in Matthew chapter 17. A man comes with his son to Jesus to ask Jesus to pray for the boy. The man says:

> *"Lord, have mercy on my son," he said. "He has seizures and is suffering greatly. He often falls into the fire or into the water. I brought him to your disciples, but they could not heal him" (Matthew 17:15-16).*

So Jesus heals the boy in a moment. The passage continues:

> *Then the disciples came to Jesus in private and asked, "Why couldn't we drive it out?"*

He replied, "Because you have so little faith. I tell you the truth, if you have faith as small as a mustard seed, you can say to this mountain, 'Move from here to there' and it will move. Nothing will be impossible for you" (Matthew 17:20-21).

It seems like Jesus is being incredibly blunt. But it also seems that the reason He's being so blunt is because what He's saying is -- to Him -- simply an established fact: If you have faith as small as a mustard seed, you can say to this mountain, 'Move from here to there' and it will move. Nothing will be impossible for you.

If it's such a fact, why don't we see it in action? The truth is, we do.

I was reading a few years ago about the power of the atomic bomb that was dropped on the city of Hiroshima, Japan. Even though an atom is one of the smallest of particles in the world, when split, an atom can produce enough energy to level an entire city within seconds. The same atomic power is at work every day at a nuclear plant near my house, powering our entire city, giving power to even the computer I'm using to type these words.

When Jesus says that something as small as

a mustard seed has enough power to move a mountain, we tend to think He's exaggerating. And yet the truth is that something even smaller than a mustard seed can move a mountain -- or several -- in an instant.

Faith in Jesus is powerful. It can move mountains. It can bring healing. It can bring repentance. It can bring new life.

Jesus didn't rebuke the demon-possessed boy, or his father, for their lack of faith. But Jesus rebuked the disciples for theirs. They had seen the power of God at work all around them, yet they faltered when putting that faith in action.

I falter, too. I don't want to, but I do. I get tired. I wonder if my prayers will ever be answered. I wonder if my faith will ever make a difference.

It's at those times that I need to renew my sense of faith and wonder in the power of Jesus Christ. It's at those times when I need to reread the stories recorded in the gospels of Matthew, Mark, Luke and John to get a fresh perspective of what faith can do. It's at those times when I need to remind myself of what the early followers of Jesus did in His name, as recorded in the book of Acts.

When I do, I'm encouraged to put my faith in Christ again, to put my faith in the power that is available to all of us who believe in His name. Power that can move mountains. Power that can restore marriages. Power that can revive broken bodies. Power that can bring people and situations and circumstances back to life.

If you need a boost in your faith today, this week, this month, read and reread what Jesus and His followers did in Matthew, Mark, Luke, John and Acts. Then put your faith to work on behalf of those you love. When you do, as Jesus promised, "Nothing will be impossible for you."

PRAYER: FATHER, OPEN MY EYES TO SEE WHAT'S POSSIBLE WHEN I PUT MY FAITH IN YOU, THEN INCREASE MY FAITH SO I CAN WATCH YOU DO IT. IN JESUS' NAME, AMEN.

Lesson 18

LOVING OTHERS
WITH FORGIVENESS

Scripture Reading: Matthew 18

One of the best ways we can express love to someone is to forgive them.

I can think of no greater expression Jesus made of His love for me than to forgive me of my sins. And it's because of His forgiveness of me that I'm able to forgive others.

Listen to how Jesus describes this connection between His forgiveness of us, and our forgiveness of others, as recorded in Matthew 18:23-35:

"Therefore, the kingdom of heaven is like a king who wanted to settle accounts with his servants. As he began the settlement, a man who owed him ten thousand talents [that is, millions of dollars] was brought to him. Since he was not able to pay, the master ordered that he and his wife and his children and all that he had be sold to repay the debt.

"The servant fell on his knees before him. 'Be patient with me,' he begged, 'and I will pay back ev-

erything.' The servant's master took pity on him, canceled the debt and let him go. "But when that servant went out, he found one of his fellow servants who owed him a hundred denarii [that is, a few dollars]. He grabbed him and began to choke him. 'Pay back what you owe me!' he demanded.

"His fellow servant fell to his knees and begged him, 'Be patient with me, and I will pay you back.'

"But he refused. Instead, he went off and had the man thrown into prison until he could pay the debt. When the other servants saw what had happened, they were greatly distressed and went and told their master everything that had happened.

"Then the master called the servant in. 'You wicked servant,' he said, 'I canceled all that debt of yours because you begged me to. Shouldn't you have had mercy on your fellow servant just as I had on you?' In anger his master turned him over to the jailers to be tortured, until he should pay back all he owed.

"This is how my heavenly Father will treat each of you unless you forgive your brother from your heart."

Jesus calls us to forgive others. This does-n't mean that we excuse them, agree with them, or ignore them. It means we forgive them. It means that we acknowledge that what they've done has hurt us, whether intentional or not, whether justified or not. It hurt. Once we acknowledge that we've been hurt, then we can forgive.

When I'm working through forgiving someone on my own, I'll sometimes write out the specific offenses I feel a person has done to me, line by line:

- *"He made a decision that cost me x amount of dollars"*
- *"He made me feel demeaned and humiliated by the way he spoke to me"*
- *"He spoke negatively about me to others, possibly turning them against me, too."*

Then I'll go through each offense, line by line, and I'll speak words of forgiveness, out loud, just for myself and God to hear. (I'll decide later whether or not it would be helpful to speak these words to someone else...only after I've truly forgiven them from my heart.) I'll say:

- *"I forgive him for making a decision that cost me x amount of dollars"*

- *"I forgive him for making me feel demeaned and humiliated by the way he spoke to me"*
- *"I forgive him for speaking negatively about me to others, possibly turning them against me, too."*

It's never easy, and I don't rush through it, because I want to make sure that my heart is right. But when I'm done, I know that I've at least begun to do what's right. Being specific helps me deal with each issue, one by one, and when I've finished going through the list, I'll throw it away. As Paul says in 1 Corinthians 13:4-5, "Love...keeps no record of wrongs."

Whatever method you choose, choose to forgive. According to Matthew 18:32-35, you'll find that when you "forgive your brother from your heart," you'll release two people from potential torment: the other person-...and yourself.

PRAYER: FATHER, HELP ME TO FORGIVE OTHERS AS YOU HAVE FORGIVEN ME. I PRAY THIS IN JESUS' NAME, AMEN.

Lesson 19

Loving Others Through Giving

Scripture Reading: Matthew 19

W hat hinders you from following Jesus completely? There's a story in the Bible about a rich young man who faced this question. He had kept the commands of God. He didn't murder. He didn't commit adultery. He didn't steal, didn't give false testimony, honored his father and mother, and loved his neighbor as himself. He asked Jesus,

"What do I still lack?"
Jesus answered, "If you want to be perfect, go, sell your possessions and give to the poor, and you will have treasure in heaven. Then come, follow me."
When the young man heard this, he went away sad, because he had great wealth. (Matthew 19:18-21).

The young man had done so much for God, yet there was still something that held him back. It makes me wonder what I might still be holding back. What is hindering me from following Jesus completely?

I remember when I felt like God was calling me into full-time ministry. I wanted to do it, felt called to do it, and was willing to give up almost anything to do it. But as I prayed through the costs, one stood out above all the others. Lana and I had saved up enough money to put a down-payment on our first house, a beautiful little house with a white picket fence. I loved that little house. I knew that if I went into full-time ministry, I might have to give it up.

As I prayed, I sensed God asking me, "Eric, do you love people more than things? Or things more than people?" I knew what I had to do. I offered the house up to God as well. Although He let me keep it for another year, I eventually had to give it up when I accepted a call to serve a church in another state. I still miss that little house, but I'm thankful that I didn't let it hold me back from doing what God called me to do.

I don't think God is as concerned about the possessions we own as He is about the possessions that own us. What is it that keeps us from following Christ completely? What holds us back from moving forward?

In order to hold on tight to God, letting Him take us wherever He wants us to go, we may have to let go of other things in our life. We may be holding onto good things, even godly things. But if they hinder us from following Christ completely, we're better off letting them go and grabbing onto Him.

Jesus concludes this passage by reminding His disciples that whatever they've given up to follow Him will not go unnoticed. Peter said to Jesus, "We have left everything to follow you! What then will there be for us?"

Jesus answered:

"I tell you the truth, at the renewal of all things, when the Son of Man sits on his glorious throne, you who have followed me will also sit on twelve thrones, judging the twelve tribes of Israel. And everyone who has left houses or brothers or sisters or father or mother or children or fields for my sake will receive a hundred times as much and will inherit eternal life" (Matthew 19:28-29).

A hundred times as much! Wow! God has so much in store for us, we can't even imagine! If what's holding us back seems so huge, imagine getting back a hundred times more! It's almost incomprehensible.

But we can't receive what God has in store for us when our fists are clenched around something else. When we open our hands to give, we're also opening them to receive.

Open your hands today. Let God use you, and what He has given you, to bless others. Then let Him bless you back in return. As Jesus told His disciples earlier: "Freely you have received, freely give" (Matthew 10:8b).

PRAYER: FATHER, OPEN MY HEART AND MY HANDS TO GIVE TO OTHERS AS YOU HAVE CALLED ME TO GIVE, SO THAT I MAY BLESS THEM, BLESS YOU, AND EVEN RECEIVE A BLESSING IN RETURN. IN JESUS' NAME, AMEN.

BECOMING A GREAT LOVER

Scripture Reading: Matthew 20

Want to become a great lover? Not just the romantic kind, but a great lover of people in general? Jesus tells us how in Matthew chapter 20.

"...whoever wants to become great among you must be your servant..." (Matthew 20:26b).

If we want to become great, we must serve others.

This is a principle Jesus taught often. It's a principle that seems to defy reason, yet we recognize its truth when we see it in action.

Mother Teresa became great, winning the Nobel Peace Prize in 1979. Yet she never sought the prize. She sought to serve others. As she saw the suffering and poverty outside the school where she taught in Calcutta, India, she sought and received permission to leave the convent school and devote herself to working among the poorest of the poor. The more she served, the more awards and distinctions she was offered, many of which she politely declined, as that was not her purpose in serving.

Jesus explained this principle to his disciples after the mother of James and John came to Jesus. She asked that Jesus would let her sons have the highest positions of honor, to sit at Jesus' right and left when He came into His kingdom. Jesus told them they didn't know what they were asking for, and that those places belonged only to those for whom they had been prepared by His Father.

Jesus explains more about this principle as the passage continues:

> *"When the ten heard about this, they were indignant with the two brothers. Jesus called them together and said, 'You know that the rulers of the Gentiles lord it over them, and their high officials exercise authority over them. Not so with you. Instead, whoever wants to become great among you must be your servant, and whoever wants to be first must be your slave— just as the Son of Man did not come to be served, but to serve, and to give his life as a ransom for many' " (Matthew 20:24-28).*

If you want to become a great lover, serve others. Although I mentioned this principle was not just about becoming a great romantic lover, the same truth applies to romance.

I've written a book called, *What God Says About Sex*. In it, I describe one of my own epiphanies regarding how God might want to use me to bless my wife, Lana. There are times when I'll look at her and ask myself, "If God were here right now, what would He do to bless her? How would He want me to use my hands, my words, my eyes, my ears, and my heart to bless her in a special way?"

Sometimes I'll sense that God wants me to caress her forehead, stroke her hair, or give her gentle kisses on her lips and cheeks. While it's nearly impossible for me not to take pleasure in this, too, my honest motivation at times like these is not to satisfy my own desires, but to let God work through me to satisfy hers.

Becoming a great lover of people, whether it involves romantic love or not, requires that we truly serve them. Bruce Wilkinson, in his book, *A Life God Rewards,* writes, "True good works are always focused on sincerely trying to improve the well-being of another."

What can you do today that would truly improve the well-being of someone you love? Is there a word you can offer, a card you can send, an email you can write? Is there something practical you can do, a trip you could make for them, a hand you could offer?

Even though you may not be seeking a reward for your good deeds, the truth is you will be rewarded for loving others. Jesus said, *"I tell you the truth, anyone who gives you a cup of water in My name...will certainly not lose his reward"* (Mark 9:41).

God wants us to become great lovers. He has shown us how. Now it's up to us to follow through.

PRAYER: FATHER, HELP ME TODAY TO BECOME THE GREAT LOVER YOU WANT ME TO BE BY SERVING OTHERS. IN JESUS' NAME, AMEN.

Lesson 21

Love Follows Through

Scripture Reading: Matthew 21

There are times when I'll be at a store with my kids and they'll ask me if we can buy something. If I know there's a special occasion coming up, like Christmas or a birthday, I might tell them, "No, we can't get that today." Then I'll go back to the store later and get what they asked for. When they finally get it, they're thrilled, and quickly forget that I had ever said no.

On the other hand, there are times when my kids will ask me for something and I'll say, "Yes, we can get that sometime." But if we never get around to getting it, they end up disappointed and frustrated, no matter how many times I might have said, "Yes, we can get that sometime."

In comparing the power of actions versus words, Ralph Waldo Emerson said: "What you do speaks so loudly that I cannot hear what you say."

Jesus sums up this idea in a parable in Matthew chapter 21. Jesus said:

> *"What do you think? There was a man who had two sons. He went to the first and said, 'Son, go and work today in the vineyard.'*
>
> *" 'I will not,' he answered, but later he changed his mind and went.*
>
> *"Then the father went to the other son and said the same thing. He answered, 'I will, sir,' but he did not go.*
>
> *"Which of the two did what his father wanted?"*
>
> *"The first," they answered.*
>
> *Jesus said to them, "I tell you the truth, the tax collectors and the prostitutes are entering the kingdom of God ahead of you. For John came to you to show you the way of righteousness, and you did not believe him, but the tax collectors and the prostitutes did. And even after you saw this, you did not repent and believe him"* (Matthew 21:28-32).

I love this story because it reminds me the importance of following through on our promises.

If we say we love God, but never repent, or never believe Him, then what good is it to say that we love Him? If we say we love our family or friends, but never follow through with the things that we promise to do for them, what good is it to say that we love them?

Jesus explained earlier the importance of letting our "Yes" be "Yes" and our "No" be "No." But here, Jesus goes to the heart of the issue. In the end, what we do matters even more than what we say.

It is what we do that will have lasting impact on those we love. It is what we do that will demonstrate our deep love and commitment to God. It is what we do that reveals how deeply committed we are in comparison to our verbal commitments of love.

This applies to everything from keeping a wedding vow to keeping a promise to a friend that we'll be at their house at 10:00. In the end, it's what we do that will speak more about our love for them than what we say.

What can you do today to follow through on a commitment you've made to God or to someone you love? How can you differentiate yourself from the religious leaders of Jesus' day who claimed to love God, but didn't follow through on what they said?

Maybe keeping your commitment is something as simple as making a phone call, filling out a job application, or keeping an appointment. Maybe it would mean taking the "next step" in a bigger issue, like saving a bit of money each week to reduce an overwhelming debt, or telling a trusted friend about a habit that's got a choke-hold on you, or opening up to your spouse about a struggle that's been keeping you from true intimacy. You may not be able to tackle the whole thing in a day, but you might be able to take a step towards it.

God wants us to follow through in our love for Him and others. In the end, it is our actions that will declare our love the loudest.

PRAYER: FATHER, SHOW ME WHAT I CAN DO TO FOLLOW THROUGH ON MY COMMITMENTS TO LOVE YOU AND LOVE OTHERS MORE. IN JESUS' NAME, AMEN.

Lesson 22

THE ULTIMATE
GOAL OF LIFE

Scripture Reading: Matthew 22

For Harry Potter fans, the week I wrote this devotional was one of the biggest double-headers of all time: the fifth movie came out the weekend before, and the seventh, and final, book in the series came out the following weekend.

Here's what I wrote:

Whatever you think of the various themes in the Harry Potter series, there's one theme that seems inarguably good: the theme of sacrificial love. In the first book, readers found out that Harry's parents, and his mother in particular, loved Harry with such a deep and sacrificial love, that even the most vile person on earth couldn't break through it to kill him. Even though Harry's parents died in the process, they succeeded in demonstrating their profound love for Harry.

Now, in the seventh and final book, readers are about to find out the answer to the question that has persisted throughout the entire series: what's going to happen to Harry Potter in his final conflict with evil? Will he live or not? It's almost guaranteed that either Harry will die, his archenemy will die, or both of them will die.

But there's another question I think readers will get an answer to this week. Although some people say there's no such thing as a dumb question, I still think that some questions are better than others! If we ask the wrong question, we'll often come to the wrong conclusion. Asking the right questions is key to life.

Beyond the question, "Will Harry live or not?" I think readers will find the answer to an even more important question: "Will Harry love or not?" In other words, "Will Harry Potter demonstrate his love for others as it was demonstrated by his parents to him?" The answer to these two questions could be entirely different, regardless of whether Harry lives or dies.

If the test of success in life is dependent on whether we live or not, none of us will pass! But if the test of success in life is whether we love or not, then all of us will have an equal chance of passing, regardless of whatever else we may do in life.

People asked Jesus all kinds of questions -- some to trap Him, others to trick Him. But one man asked Jesus a question that was so wise Jesus said to him, "You are not far from the kingdom of God."

The question was this: "Of all the commandments, which is the most important?"

"The most important one," answered Jesus, "is this: 'Hear, O Israel, the Lord our God, the Lord is one. Love the Lord your God with all your heart and with all your soul and with all your mind and with all your strength.' The second is this: 'Love your neighbor as yourself.' There is no commandment greater than these" (Mark 12:29-31 and Matthew 22:37-40).

The man had asked the right question. And Jesus gave a brilliant response.

We may have heard Jesus's answer so often that we don't realize the incredible power of His words. Jesus says that the goal of everything in life -- everything -- boils down to whether or not we love God with all our heart, soul, mind and strength; and whether or not we love others as ourselves. Love is the ultimate goal of life.

Will Harry Potter live or not? I don't know. I'm curious, but I'm even more curious if Harry Potter will love or not. Will he demonstrate his love to others as it has been demonstrated to him? The answer to that question will determine the success or failure of Harry Potter's life. And it's the same question that will determine the success or failure of our lives.

Will we love God and others as God has loved us? Will we succeed in life, by demonstrating our love for others as Christ demonstrated His when He gave His life for us? If our answer to these questions is a resounding "YES!" then it won't matter what else we might do in life. We will have succeeded in the ultimate goal of life, the goal of love.

PRAYER: FATHER, HELP ME DEMONSTRATE MY LOVE FOR YOU AND OTHERS AS YOU HAVE DEMONSTRATED IT TO ME. IN JESUS' NAME, AMEN.

Lesson 23

LOVING PEOPLE, NOT JUST WORDS

Scripture Reading: Matthew 23

The day I put my faith in Jesus was the same day I put my faith in the Bible, from which I learned about Jesus. I fell in love with both on the same day.

When people talk about how much they love the Bible, they're not just talking about a book from which they've learned much, they're also talking about a Person from whom they've learned much.

I suppose it's like a young lover who takes a picture of his beloved out of his wallet and tenderly kisses the image. It's not the picture that the young man's in love with, but a person whose image is represented by the picture. If his love for the picture ever began to surpass his love for the person, then we'd know that something had started to go wrong.

Believe it or not, the same thing can happen to those of us who love the Bible. When our love for the Word of God begins to supersede our love for God -- and our love for the people of God about whom the words were written -- then we know something has started to go wrong.

Jesus criticized the religious leaders of His day for this very thing. They claimed to love the Word of God, and even gave the appearance of following the commands found in it to the "T." But Jesus saw their hearts; He saw that they weren't motivated by their love for others, but by how they appeared to others. It was a subtle difference that produced drastically different results than God had intended.

Jesus didn't condemn these leaders for what they were teaching, for they were teaching the Word of God. But He did condemn then for how they put those words into practice. He said:

"The teachers of the law and the Pharisees sit in Moses' seat. So you must obey them and do everything they tell you. But do not do what they do, for they do not practice what they preach. They tie up heavy loads and put them on men's shoulders, but they themselves are not willing to lift a finger to

move them. Everything they do is done for men to see..." (Matthew 23:2-5).

Jesus goes on to denounce the actions of those leaders in some of the strongest words in the Bible, calling them hypocrites, snakes, vipers, and sons of hell. Yikes! I don't want to be like that! I hope you don't either! So what can we do instead?

Jesus tells us in the same passage. For starters, we're to do the opposite of what the teachers of the law and the Pharisees were doing! He doesn't want us to just preach to others, but to practice what we preach. When we give godly advice to others, we're not just to walk away and say, "I've told you what to do, now good luck." He wants us to at least lift a finger -- and more -- to help them to do it.

If someone's struggling with an addiction, rather than just telling them it's wrong, offer to be their accountability partner. If someone's considering a divorce, rather than just telling them to try to work it out with their spouse, help them to work it out with their spouse. If someone's going under financially, rather than just telling them to work out a budget, help them to work out a budget. I'm preaching to myself, too! It's often easier to tell people what they should do than to help them to do it, which is why I'm studying these "lessons in love"!

Our motivation in sharing God's Word must always be love -- saying and doing things that will truly benefit those we're trying to help, whether anyone sees our good deeds or not.

If we claim to love the Word of God, we must also love the people of God about whom the words are written. To do anything less would be like falling in love with a piece of paper with some ink on it.

PRAYER: FATHER, HELP ME TO LOVE YOUR PEOPLE, REMEMBERING THAT YOUR WORDS WERE WRITTEN BECAUSE OF YOUR GREAT LOVE FOR THEM. IN JESUS' NAME, AMEN.

Lesson 24

Don't Let Your Love Grow Cold

Scripture Reading: Matthew 24

Jesus tells us many things that will happen as the time gets closer to His return. Most of them I can't do anything about: famines, earthquakes, wars and rumors of war.

But there's one thing Jesus mentions in Matthew chapter 24 that I can do: don't let my love grow cold. Jesus says:

> *"Because of the increase of wickedness, the love of most will grow cold, but he who stands firm to the end will be saved" (Matthew 24:12:13).*

I can see how our love could grow cold. As the world approaches its grand finale, with rampant, widespread destruction, it would be easy to become embittered, frustrated, heartsick and fearful. I can see how people could turn away from God, and turn away from each other.

But Jesus gives us the key to surviving those times. And it's really the key to surviving whatever we're facing right now, too. The key is this: "Don't let your love grow cold."

When your love grows cold, the end really has come. When your love grows cold, that's the end of joy, the end of relationships, the end of happiness, the end of hope. At all costs, whatever it takes, we need to keep our love alive. Our love for God, and our love for others.

I was speaking to a group one time about what to do when people treat us poorly. The answer, I suggested, was to "Love 'em more." What should we do when people run away from us? "Love 'em more." What should we do when people break our hearts and disappoint us? "Love 'em more."

One of the people in the group came up to me the next day. She said she loved that message on "Love me more." Whenever people would treat her poorly, she'd remind them that they're supposed to "Love me more." She was joking, of course, having gotten the two key letters backwards, turning "em" into "me." It's a minor change with major ramifications. When things get rough in relationships, we expect others to "Love me more." But what God calls us to do is to "Love them more," or as I put it, "Love 'em more."

This is a message that we don't have to wait to put into practice until the end of the world as we know it. It's a message that we can start practicing today, so when the end comes, we'll be ready. In fact, we're closer to Jesus' return today than ever before. We're not lacking in famines, earthquakes, wars and rumors of war. If there's a time to put our love into practice, we need to start "practicing" now.

None of us know when the day of His return will come. Although there will be signs, it will come suddenly. People will be eating and drinking as usual, marrying and giving in marriage up until that day. *"Two men will be in the field; one will be taken and the other left. Two women will be grinding with a hand mill; one will be taken and the other left"* (Matthew 24:40-41).

The grand finale of life will come upon us in an instant. What can we do about it? 1) Don't be surprised when these things happen. Jesus says, *"but see to it that you are not alarmed. Such things must happen, but the end is still to come"*

(Matthew 24:6b). 2) Don't let your love grow cold.

How can we keep our love from growing cold? By fanning the flames of our love.

- *When people hurt you or mistreat you, "Love 'em more."*
- *When people leave you or forsake you, "Love 'em more."*
- *When people sin against you or hate you, "Love 'em more."*

Just like Jesus did for us when people hurt and mistreated Him, left and forsook Him, sinned against and hated Him. He just loved 'em more.

Even to the very end, the thing that will save the day will be love. As wickedness increases all around us, we need to do what Jesus did : "Love 'em more."

PRAYER: FATHER, HELP ME TO LOVE OTHERS MORE, EVEN AS -- AND ESPECIALLY WHEN -- WE SEE THE END APPROACHING. IN JESUS' NAME, AMEN.

Lesson 25

LOVE IS
PREPARED

Scripture Reading: Matthew 25

I was reading the Parable of the Talents one day when my life took a radical turn. The parable is a story in Matthew chapter 25 where Jesus tells about a man who gave three of his servants varying amounts of talents -- a unit of money that was worth more than $1,000.

You're probably familiar with the story: the man gave the first servant five talents, the second servant two talents, and the third servant one talent. Then the man went on a journey.

Quite awhile later, the man came back to see what each servant had done with his talents. Two of the servants had put their talents to use, making a good return on the man's investment. Each was rewarded by their master with these words:

" Well done, good and faithful servant! You have

been faithful with a few things; I will put you in charge of many things. Come and share your master's happiness!"

But the third servant had buried his talent and was rebuked as wicked and lazy. Even what he had was taken away from him, and he was thrown out into the darkness.

Of course, after reading the story, I wanted to be like the first two servants, not like the third.

Wondering how I was doing with the "talents" God had given me, I began to write a question in my journal. "Lord, am I using the gifts you've given me?" I was surprised when the answer I heard back was a clear and simple, "No."

Wow! I thought I was doing pretty good! I was working hard at my job, involved in some Bible studies at church, and so on. But I knew that if this really was God speaking to me, I wanted to listen up. I didn't want to be like the wicked, lazy servant in the story who didn't put his talents to use.

"Lord, what do you want me to do?" I wrote.

I felt God answered: "I told them to make a return on what I gave them."

So I began to list out a few of my talents, asking God how I could make better use of them for Him. One week later, I quit my secular job and went into full-time ministry.

Jesus told two other parables in Matthew chapter 25, both of which talk about preparing for Christ's return. Jesus doesn't want us to be surprised when that day comes. He doesn't want us to fall asleep waiting for His return. He doesn't want us to bury our talents in the ground. He doesn't want us to neglect the needs of those around us.

He wants us to put our gifts to use to the fullest, to be ready when He comes back.

It doesn't mean we all need to be in "full-time ministry." But it does mean that we're to use the gifts He's given us to work towards His purposes on the earth. Whether it's giving food to the hungry, drinks to the thirsty, or clothes to the naked. Whether it's looking after those who are sick, visiting those who are in prison, or caring for our children or parents. Whether it's cooking or sewing, teaching or preaching, singing or praying.

When Jesus comes back, He wants us to be

prepared for His return. Not because He wants us to work our way into heaven. But because He wants us to make a good return on His investment. He's given us all kinds of gifts, and He wants us to use them to the fullest, to accomplish all that He has created us to do.

Take inventory of some of the gifts God has given you. Ask Him how you can use those gifts for Him. Let's pray that one day we'll all hear Him say, "Well done, good and faithful servant! You have been faithful with a few things; I will put you in charge of many things. Come and share your master's happiness!"

PRAYER: FATHER, HELP ME TO MAKE A GOOD RETURN ON THE GIFTS YOU'VE GIVEN ME, FOR MY SAKE, FOR YOURS, AND FOR THOSE WHO WILL BE TOUCHED AS A RESULT. IN JESUS' NAME, AMEN.

LAVISH
LOVE

Scripture Reading: Matthew 26

I've read the story in Matthew chapter 26 many times about the woman who poured out a jar of very expensive perfume onto Jesus's head. I've always been impressed by the woman's action, and by Jesus's response to it.

But it wasn't until recently that I've seen the story from God's perspective, which has deepened my appreciation for it even more.

In case you haven't read it, or just need a refresher, here's the story:

While Jesus was in Bethany in the home of a man known as Simon the Leper, a woman came to him with an alabaster jar of very expensive perfume, which she poured on his head as he was reclining at the table. When the disciples saw this, they were indignant. "Why this waste?" they asked. "This perfume could have been sold at a high price and the money given to the poor."

Aware of this, Jesus said to them, "Why are you bothering this woman? She has done a beautiful thing to me. The poor you will always have with you, but you will not always have me. When she poured this perfume on my body, she did it to prepare me for burial. I tell you the truth, wherever this gospel is preached throughout the world, what she has done will also be told, in memory of her" (Matthew 26:6-13).

I love this woman's lavish love for Jesus. I'm sure she knew the value of her gift. She didn't see it as wasteful, but as totally appropriate for the one who was to receive it.

I also love Jesus's response to this gift. He wasn't bothered that someone poured out such a lavish expression of love upon Him. He was, after all, the one who turned water into wine -- and not just any wine, but the best. He understood what it meant to lavish love upon others.

But what I love even more about this story is the lavish love of God for His Son displayed in this act. From God's perspective, it's almost as if God wanted to pour out a special measure of His love to Jesus, so He moved on the heart of a woman who had a very expensive jar of perfume, allowing her to be His hands to His Son. He put in her heart the willingness to pick up her alabaster jar and pour it out on Jesus's head.

God knew what Jesus was about to undergo. Jesus knew what He was about to undergo. If there was ever a time where Jesus might have doubted His Father's love for Him, it was in the upcoming days of mocking, beating, and being nailed to a cross. This demonstration of love was as if God wanted to assure Jesus of His love yet one more time, moving on the heart of a woman who could pour out just such an expression. It was an act of lavish love, not only from the woman, but from God Himself, given through the woman.

Why is this so important to point out? Because God may want to do the same thing through you for others. He may want to show someone His lavish love, and in order to do that, He may move on your heart to display it. We all have an alabaster jar of some kind. It may not be an expensive perfume, but it may be just as valuable to the person receiving it.

Maybe it's a gift of time, of attention, of

writing a song, of serving with our hands. Maybe it's a gift of money, giving something that may or may not mean much to us, but will certainly mean something special to the recipient. Maybe it's a gift of an item, an object of value, something that would mean the world to someone else.

Sometimes love is outlandishly lavish. But sometimes, from God's perspective, it's just the kind of love that He wants us to pour out on others.

PRAYER: FATHER, HELP ME TO BE WILLING TO SHOW YOUR LAVISH LOVE TO OTHERS, DEMONSTRATING YOUR LOVE FOR THEM IN TANGIBLE WAYS. IN JESUS' NAME, AMEN.

Lesson 27

A Tale Of Two Deaths

Scripture Reading: Matthew 27

Two of the most famous deaths ever recorded take place in Matthew chapter 27. Interestingly, even though these two men had starkly different lives and deaths, the way each of them died was a reflection of the way they lived. And in their deaths, there's a lesson for how we can live and die better, too.

The chapter opens with the death of Judas, the disciple who betrayed Jesus with a kiss. His sad death is a reflection of his sad life. Just days before, he had watched contemptuously as a woman poured out a jar of expensive perfume onto Jesus's head. He complained, *"Why wasn't this perfume sold and the money given to the poor? It was worth a year's wages."*

The Bible goes on to say, *"He did not say this because he cared about the poor but because he was a thief; as keeper of the money bag, he used to help himself to what was put into it." (John 12:5-6).*

It was this event that caused Judas to go to the chief priests and ask, " *What are you willing to give me if I hand him over to you?' So they counted out for him thirty silver coins. From then on Judas watched for an opportunity to hand him over*" *(Matthew 26:15-16).*

It was almost as if following Jesus was simply a means to an end for Judas. As long as the money was coming in, he was glad to follow. But when he saw this "wasteful" display of money by the woman, and Jesus's apparent indifference to the finances involved, Judas began to look for another way to profit from the situation.

Sadly, when he realized his mistake, betraying an innocent man to death for thirty pieces of silver, it was too late. He couldn't live with what he had done, so he took his own life. It seems that money was what Judas lived for, and money was what Judas died for.

Contrast this story with the other story of death in this chapter, the death of Jesus.

Having been betrayed by Judas, Jesus was taken to be sentenced. Yet when accused, the Bible says, *"But Jesus made no reply, not even to a single charge -- to the great amazement of the governor"* *(Matthew 27:14).*

Jesus knew what He had to do. Although He had agonized in prayer, asking God if there was any other way to do what He had to do, Jesus was willing to follow God no matter what. Jesus had always lived for others. Now He was about to die for others, too.

Taking His last breath on the cross, Jesus called out in a loud voice, *"Father, into your hands I commit my spirit"* (Luke 23:46).

The deaths of these two men couldn't have been more different. Judas took his life because of sin. Jesus gave up His life because of love. The difference can be seen when looking into their hearts.

When you look into the heart of love, you'll find selflessness. When you look into the heart of sin, you'll find selfishness.

If we want to love like Jesus loved, we've got to live like Jesus lived -- then be willing to die like Jesus died. In doing so, we'll find true life. As Jesus Himself said,

> *"For whoever wants to save his life will lose it, but whoever loses his life for Me will find it."* (Matthew 16:25).

I pray that when people look into your

heart and mine, that they'll see that our hearts are willing to die for the same things that we're willing to live for.

I pray that our hearts would overflow with a love that is eager to live for others, give to others, and even to die for others when that time comes.

I'm not expecting to die anytime soon, and you may not be either. But I pray that when that day comes, our deaths would be a reflection of our lives, a reflection of the heart of Jesus.

PRAYER: FATHER, HELP ME TO GIVE UP MY LIFE OF SELFISHNESS SO THAT I CAN GIVE OUT A LIFE OF SELFLESSNESS. IN JESUS' NAME, AMEN.

FIT FOR
WHAT?

Scripture Reading: Matthew 28

Why do we go to church? Read the Bible? Pray? Listen to sermons? Read devotionals?

Why? To grow. To be stronger in our faith. To help us through difficult times. To find God's answers for specific questions on our heart. Certainly it's for each of those things.

But there's more! God has more in mind for us from all of our reading, studying and praying than simply our own spiritual growth. He wants us to be spiritually fit. The question is, fit for what?

Jesus tells us the answer in Matthew chapter 28, verses 18 through 20. In this passage, often referred to as "The Great Commission," Jesus gives His final instructions to His disciples -- instructions that apply to us today as well, as followers of Jesus Christ. Jesus said:

"All authority in heaven and on earth has been given to me. Therefore go and make disciples of all nations, baptizing them in the name of the Father and of the Son and of the Holy Spirit, and teaching them to obey everything I have commanded you. And surely I am with you always, to the very end of the age" (Matthew 28:18-20).

If all of our reading and studying and praying was solely to help us grow for our own sakes, we'd be like a body builder who works out for years to compete in a contest, but never actually uses his muscles to lift anything "in the real world." They would certainly be fit, but fit for what?

I'm not against bodybuilding, and I wish I had some of those muscles myself! But in reading Jesus' words, I'm convicted that sometimes we as Christians can focus so much on the workout that we forget why we're working out.

Our spiritual workouts may include Bible studies, quiet times, and memorizing scripture, all of which are great and helpful in their own right. But in the end, Jesus wants us to put what we've learned into practice, serving others as He served them. Baptizing others as He baptized them. Teaching others as He taught them.

How can we do that today? How can we use our gifts to make disciples of all nations? How can we encourage people to get baptized? How can we teach others to obey all that Christ has commanded us?

The list is endless of how God creatively uses people to join Him in His work.

I know a woman who wondered how God could use her to fulfill this command. She liked to swim...but what could she do with that? Then a neighbor boy asked her if she would teach him how to swim in her backyard pool. She agreed to do it, on the condition that he memorize a Bible verse every time he came for a lesson. He did it, loved it, and soon brought his friends. They, too, began taking swimming lessons and memorizing Scripture. Within a few years, this woman was holding her swimming classes at a public pool, because over a hundred kids were coming each day to learn how to swim and memorize Scripture.

I have an aunt who loves to cook, but how could that help fulfill The Great Commission?

Over the years, she has hosted hundreds of pastors, Bible teachers, missionaries, students, neighbors, friends and relatives in her home, giving them a physical, as well as a spiritual lift as they've come through her home.

How might He want to use you this week, this month, this year? What do you love doing? What do you have a passion for? What are you skilled at that could be tweaked, even just a little, to help bring others into the kingdom of God?

God has gifted you, certainly because He loves you, but also because He wants to love others through you.

Keep asking God how you can get into the best spiritual shape possible. He wants each of us to be as fit as we can be...fit for all that He wants to do through us in the days ahead.

PRAYER: FATHER, HELP ME TO FIND CREATIVE WAYS TO PUT MY SPIRITUAL FITNESS TO USE FOR YOU AND YOUR KINGDOM. IN JESUS' NAME, AMEN.

Conclusion

THE GREATEST OF THESE

Scripture Reading: 1 Corinthians 13:1-13

Today we've come to the end of our study of the book of Matthew. I hope you've enjoyed learning how to love God, love others, and love ourselves more by seeing how Jesus did each of those things.

Here are some of the things I've learned about love from the life of Jesus, one from each of Matthew's 28 chapters:

1) Those who have been forgiven much love much
2) Love starts by seeing others as God sees them
3) Love continues by seeing how much God loves people even before they were born
4) Love sometimes requires that we call people to repent from things that are destroying them
5) We're called to love everyone, even our enemies
6) We're called to make sure our motives are right, by sometimes doing loving acts in secret
7) The Golden Rule is still golden: God wants us to do to others as we would have them do to us

8) *We can love others by praying for their healing*

9) *We can love others by bringing them to Jesus*

10) *We can let God's perfect love drive out our fears*

11) *We can love others by helping them through their doubts*

12) *Love requires us to do right, even when threatened*

13) *People sometimes respond better to our loving words when spoken in parables*

14) *Love is balanced between prayer and action*

15) *Love often requires persistence*

16) *Love often requires dying to our own desires*

17) *Love often requires asking for more faith to see the lives of our friends changed*

18) *Love forgives*

19) *Love gives*

20) *Love serves*

21) *Love follows through*

22) *Our success in life is not determined by how long we live, but by how much we love*

23) *Our love for God's Word should be directly related to our love for God's people*

24) *When tempted to let our love grow cold, we must determine to love others more*

25) *Love is prepared*

26) *Love is lavish*

27) Love is sacrificial
28) Love goes to the ends of the earth

There's a lot we can learn from reading the Bible. There's a lot we can learn from praying. But in the end, all of our reading and praying won't matter unless we express what we've learned in love. Theology matters, but only to the extent that it influences our ability to love.

I love the way Oliver Thomas puts it: "Authentic religion is not a theology test. It's a love test."

If what we learn doesn't influence what we do, all of our learning is in vain.

The Apostle Paul expressed it well when he wrote:

"If I speak in the tongues of men and of angels, but have not love, I am only a resounding gong or a clanging cymbal. If I have the gift of prophecy and can fathom all mysteries and all knowledge, and if I have a faith that can move mountains, but have not love, I am nothing. If I give all I possess to the poor and surrender my body to the flames, but have not love, I gain nothing" (1 Corinthians 13:1-4).

Paul continues his passage on love by giving one of the most useful summaries of love found not only in the whole Bible, but perhaps in all the writings of the world. He continues:

"Love is patient, love is kind. It does not envy, it does not boast, it is not proud. It is not rude, it is not self-seeking, it is not easily angered, it keeps no record of wrongs. Love does not delight in evil but rejoices with the truth. It always protects, always trusts, always hopes, always perseveres. Love never fails" (1 Corinthians 13:4-7).

Paul concludes his famous passage on love by expressing the greatest things God looks for in a person, the greatest measure of every one of our lives. The same words that I'd like to conclude with as well:

"And now these three remain: faith, hope and love. But the greatest of these is love" (1 Corinthians 13:13).

PRAYER: FATHER, HELP ME TO KEEP LOVE AT THE FOREFRONT OF EVERYTHING ELSE I DO IN LIFE. IN JESUS' NAME, AMEN.

About The Author

Described by *USA Today* as "a new breed of evangelist," Eric Elder is an ordained pastor, songwriter and the creator of *The Ranch,* a faith-boosting website that attracts thousands of visitors each month at www.TheRanch.org.

Eric is also an inspirational writer and speaker, having written about spiritual issues for publications like Billy Graham's *Decision Magazine,* and spoken about loving others at national conferences like the *Exodus International Freedom Conference.*

Eric has also written a book focusing specifically on romantic love called *What God Says About Sex,* which has helped many to discover and put into practice what God says about one of the most intimate forms of love.

To listen to, download or order more inspiring resources, please visit:

www.TheRanch.org

2894101

Made in the USA